Be A Better Partner™
Handbook

By Debbie and Paul Lamb

Be A Better Partner™ Handbook

Copyright © 2006 by: Debbie & Paul Lamb,

Lambs On Love Inc.

P.O. Box 5426, Vallejo, CA 94591

www.beabetterpartner.com

Email: info@beabetterpartner.com

ISBN: 978-1-4303-0862-1

First Edition

About The Authors:

Debbie and Paul Lamb are the co-founders of Lambs On Love, and organization devoted to successful relationship building. They don't claim to have all the answers to a great relationship, but they do have a few good clues, based on a happy, loving partnership.

We dedicate this book to Keith.

We are thankful for many people and experiences in our lives. But it was you who had the greatest impact on our relationship. We are forever grateful for the gift of having had you in our lives, however brief.

From the bottom of our hearts, we thank you.

Thanks and Acknowledgements

⦿ First of all, thank you to Isabella &
Michaela for keeping us young and
reminding us every day of our priorities.
Thanks to John McCarthy for the great
photographs. Thanks to Jim & Joann
Lamb for your fine example and support,
and an edit or two. Thanks Matthew &
Kristina Heim for your vision and thanks to
all of the therapists, counselors – both
formal & informal – who have helped us
stay on course.

⦿ And a special thanks to our Partner
Guinea Pigs: Doug & Lee Stein; Jessy &
Angelica Gonzalez; Annette & Earl
Hampton; and John & Jeanne McCarthy.

⦿ And thanks to both of our families for
their love.

Table Of Contents

Our Short Story

There once was a boy and a girl who met and fell in love. They were very different people and had lots of quirks. She was a sarcastic, strong-willed, people person...and a power shopper. He was a moody dreamer, who enjoyed singing loudly...in the shower.

Despite their differences, and lacking any formal relationship training, they decided to move in together, and got married.

They had a great wedding, with all of their family and friends, and a romantic honeymoon on a cruise in the Mediterranean.

They had two kids, bought a house, and settled down for the long haul.

Along the way, they realized a few things that hadn't seemed that important before. They realized how truly different they were from each other. She liked to stay home and he liked to get out. She liked to watch TV, and he liked to read books. He liked to exercise, and she would rather be eating chocolate. He was scared to death meeting new people, and she was entirely at ease in a room full of strangers.

They also started to pay more attention to the little things that bugged them about each other. She hated those little hairs he left in the bathroom sink after shaving, and he would go ballistic over her leaving little piles of clutter around the house that never seemed to get cleaned up. She wanted the heat turned up when he was already sweating. He would occasionally shock her and sleep in his clothes, and she would come to bed night after night and shock him with her frigid toes up against his warm body.

After ten years of emotional battles, tears, and some serious counseling, they realized something else. They realized there was a powerful reason they had fallen in love and gotten married. The reason is that, despite their differences, they are without a doubt the best thing that ever happened to each other.

From him she learned to widen her horizons, let go of her sarcasm, and learn to appreciate the meaning of the term: quiet time. From her he learned the importance of family, why talking things out was better than steaming silently, and the therapeutic value of watching crappy TV shows.

They learned together that their differences could actually be complementary rather than antagonistic. They learned that cherishing each other is a far cry from just compromising and putting up with each other. They learned that a healthy, passionate relationship means getting to a place where you can't stand the thought of *not* being together. But how the heck do you do that?

A Couple of Ideas for Relationship Building

The experts will tell you a lot of things to help improve your relationship, primarily to get a good therapist. If you have a good therapist, great! But we are here to suggest an additional idea, and it won't cost you $100 plus per hour:

HAVE FUN!!! Yes, outrageous, passionate, spontaneous, goofy, improvised, out-of-this-world FUN. Practicing the art of relationship building doesn't have to be a burden. On the contrary, you should have as much fun as possible learning (or re-learning) to honor, love, and support your partner.

Of course, it's hard to have fun when you don't necessarily feel very happy with each other, are perhaps a little rusty, or are not sure where to start. So we offer you a simple way to get started, a way that can work for anyone, regardless of where your relationship is at.

Our secret: Practice your relationship building one month at a time. Take it step by step and in a way that is simple and doesn't require you to completely alter your life or lifestyle. All it requires is for you both to put aside a couple of hours each month and to follow along with a series of different themes for each month that are designed to encourage you to have fun while enhancing your relationship. You yourselves can decide how much or how little you want to invest in it, depending on your own situation.

About the Book

This book is a simple collection of what we, Debbie and Paul Lamb, have learned in becoming a happy couple. Some of these things we have learned the hard way, while others have been taught to us by some really smart and loving people. What you will find here is a collection of easy, practical – and most importantly - *fun* things that we do to keep our relationship moving forward.

Along with monthly themes and activities, we have also included plenty of examples from our own experiences and some items from our personal archives.

We don't claim to have all the answers, and we don't have PhDs or extensive research studies to present in these pages. But what we do have is a lot of love for each other. And we do know that we will be spending the rest of our lives with each other and are feeling really stoked about it!

Hopefully this book and our BE A BETTER PARTNER™ wall calendar will help you get closer with your own partner. Who knows... you might even fall in love all over again?

How to Use this Book

1. Read a chapter (just a few pages each) a month, which should take about 15 minutes or so.
2. Select the activities from each chapter that you will do each month.
3. Use your accompanying Be A Better Partner™ calendar or use an existing calendar to write down and track selected activities.

Best Practices

1. Read each chapter together, in bed at night, for example. (reading it when you are lying flat after a REALLY long day is NOT recommended, however)

2. Read a chapter together during a date night (you do have a date night, don't you?)

3. Take a look at your calendar every day or two, just to see where you are and what's next.

4. Use the online calendar at www.beabetterpartner.com to sync your Be A Better Partner™ wall calendar with your electronic personal or business calendar (on Outlook, iCalender, etc.). You can also receive reminders about selected activities on your computer, cell phone or other mobile device.

5. Have a joint celebration at the completion of each month's chapter and activities.

6. Tell your friends about what you are planning or have done, and see what ideas they have.

7. Share your own experiences and learn from others in the larger Be A Better Partner™ community. Tell us what is working in your relationship at www.beabetterpartner.com. Here you can also learn about and contribute additional fun and meaningful partner activities, services, etc.

Chapter 1

Adventure Month

Ladies and Gentlemen, boys and girls, welcome to the beginning of your adventure together with, you guessed it, Adventure Month. This month we will be focusing on being crazy, trying new things, and taking some risks, together.

Remember the first time you met, or when you first realized that your partner was "the one"? Remember how you felt like you could scale the highest mountain, and you wanted nothing more than to be with your "other"? Well, take a moment to think and feel about that, and then ask yourself a few questions:

1. What have we not done in a really long time that we used to love to do together?
2. What have we never done that we would still REALLY like to do?
3. What could I do with my partner that she/he would also totally enjoy?
4. What can we do together THIS MONTH?

Now, just to be clear, you don't need to plan a trip to go backpacking through Europe together – although that would be great. The most important thing is that you think of things that are relatively easy to arrange, fit within your budget and timetable, and are doable. At the same time, try not to limit yourself by all of those distracting adult voices in your head: "I can't afford"..."I don't have time to"..."I am just too tired to..." etc.

Stay focused on that feeling of first falling in love, and pick your adventures based on what *those* feelings tell you to do.*

Then choose at least one thing that you will commit to doing together, and decide on who is going to make the arrangements – RIGHT NOW! Try to share the planning, arranging, and preparing if it makes sense to do that. This reinforces that each partner adventure is as a joint undertaking, not a solo trip.

Second, take some time to choose at least one adventure that you will do individually, away from your partner. Why? Because as much as we want to work on a joint adventure during this month, we still need to acknowledge that we have individual needs for adventure that don't always and shouldn't always include your other half. It's perfectly fine to acknowledge that, don't you think?

The more that we can step back and be adventurous, even individually, the greater our chances that we will awaken a passion for adventure in all things in life – something that will nourish and ideally help to revitalize the adventure we call a relationship!

Steps:
1. Talk about some adventures you would like to take together and individually.
2. Select which joint and individual adventures you would like to pursue this month.
3. Write them down on your Be A Better Partner™ wall calendar or log on to our online calendar through www.beabetterparner.com, where you can sync electronic calendars on your computer, personal digital assistant, or cell phone. The electronic calendar also allows you to set up email or text messaging reminders so that you don't forget important dates.

OK, here are some Activity Ideas** to get you started:
   ◉ Have a picnic in your living room.

- ◉ Take a dance class or martial arts class together.
- ◉ Go hiking at a place you have never been.
- ◉ Go to an inexpensive motel and spend the night.
- ◉ Take a ropes challenge course together.
- ◉ Create a scavenger hunt in your neighborhood or home for your partner.
- ◉ Go to an amusement park or area attraction for the day.
- ◉ Plan and book an exotic vacation.
- ◉ Join a sports team together.
- ◉ Take a balloon ride.
- ◉ Volunteer to do a community project together.
- ◉ Go to a bus, subway or train station and take a trip without first deciding where you will go.
- ◉ Go skiing, sledding or waterskiing.
- ◉ Check out www.beabetterpartner.com to learn about or share additional ideas.

*Please note that the authors of this book are in no way responsible for broken bones, bruised egos, or multiple trips to the Emergency Room as a result of YOUR chosen adventure activities. We encourage you to be adventurous, NOT stupid!

**IMPORTANT: All adventures should NOT include any kids if you have them. This is YOUR time as a couple only.

From the Real Life Archives:

You've done a good thing.

And I, for one, look forward to whatever
happens next on
our Great Adventure!

I have faith in you.

And us.

Chapter 2

Surprise Me Month

Surprise, surprise... it's time to expect the unexpected this month. Yes, let's spice things up with some fun surprises. Why surprises? Because one of the problems that most couples face is getting into a predictable pattern that can lead to boredom. So, think "anti-boredom" and begin planning some good stuff.

By the way, a good surprise doesn't necessarily have to be a surprise party that takes months of planning. And they don't necessarily have to be things like diamond earrings or a Harley-Davidson that cost a lot of money. They don't necessarily need to be "things" at all.

Because you only have a month to do your respective surprise(s) for you partner, remember to try to keep it simple, but filled with meaning. A good surprise doesn't have to be grandiose; it just has to communicate the idea that "I was thinking of you, and I took the time to do something for you that I thought would make you happy."

Debbie and Paul's Favorite Surprises:

Debbie: "As goofy as it sounds, one of the best surprises I received from Paul was arriving home one evening after a long commute, to the smell of dinner cooking in the kitchen! As the primary cook in our home, this surprise was the best gift I could have received at that moment in time. I'll never forget it."

Paul: "A favorite surprise of mine was a video that I got for my birthday. Debbie had asked my family and friends to each take a moment and video a greeting and birthday wish. She then secretly put everything together on one tape and I got to see all of my favorite people, scattered around the country, on my birthday. I was blown away!"

Now, let's get started...

Steps:

1. First, think of some of your favorite surprises and share them with each other.
2. Ask each other "what kind of surprise do you like the best?"
3. Take a minute to think to yourself about what you could realistically do THIS month as a small or large surprise.
4. Write down your ideas on a piece of paper but don't show it to your partner.

Once you have an idea or two you can choose to write down some generic "surprise me" days, without disclosing any particulars, on your Be a Better Partner™ wall calendar. Of course you can also choose not to write anything down at all, preferring instead to maintain a true element of surprise during Surprise Me Month. Finally, you can also go to www.beabetterpartner.com and enter in some dates privately on our electronic calendar, and then sync those dates with your own personal or business calendar so that your partner will not know about them.

Activity Ideas:

- Surprise your partner at work and take her/him to lunch.
- Plan a secret evening when one partner is completely in the dark, and anywhere they get taken is brand new.
- Slip some money into your spouse's purse/wallet with a note and instructions on a fun task to be done on a chosen day.
- Put a love letter under your partner's pillow, in their briefcase, etc.
- Put a sign or poster on the door welcoming them home from work, from a trip, etc.
- Send a loving email to your partner at work or text message them a short love note.
- Send an audio or video clip to your partner with a special message.
- Clean your partner's car – or "pimp" it out one day.
- Bake cookies or a favorite food.
- Draw a surprise bath and light candles for the gift of some quiet time.
- Surprise your partner by doing an unexpected good deed for a relative, friend, or neighbor.
- Go to www.beabetterpartner.com for additional ideas or to share your own.

From the Real Life Archives:

10 Things I most love about Debbie

1. She ~~is~~ values people more than she does things
2. Her ~~beautiful~~ amazing smile
3. She is who she appears to be and calls it like she sees it
4. She takes care of stray dogs (including this one)
5. She is a wonderful and dedicated mother
6. She laughs at my stupid jokes
7. She doesn't take life too seriously
8. She doesn't let me take myself too seriously
9. She gets better ~~~~ and healthier with Age
10. She is a beautiful woman and makes me feel proud to be with her

Chapter 3

Be Good to Yourself Month

Now that you have experienced some adventures together and worked hard at pleasantly surprising your partner, it's time for a little breather. Yes, you deserve a break today...and for the rest of Be Good to Yourself Month. This month's theme is all about taking some time to do something nice for yourself. We are not suggesting that this is an opportunity for you to abandon your partner and embark on a solo cruise to the Caribbean for two weeks. Rather, we are suggesting that you take to heart the importance of celebrating yourself.

How does this relate to enhancing your relationship? Well, we have learned that as different people we need and deserve time away from each other on occasion to do our own thing. We have found that this simple practice of time away helps to rejuvenate us and teaches us to be accepting of each others' right to private space. It also helps us to recognize our own legitimate wants and needs, giving us permission to develop a stronger sense of self that will lead to greater individual happiness.

Here is an opportunity to be nice to yourself in a healthy and encouraging fashion...without any guilt or judgments attached!

Yes, this month you have permission to line up some enjoyable activities for yourself and not worry about what your partner thinks. In fact, you should come at this by encouraging your partner to do whatever he/she wants, and not be judgmental.

Steps:

⦾ Sit down and think about some things that you enjoy doing that don't include your partner. Remember not to worry about whether your partner will approve of them or not. Also, try to choose things that you don't often do or perhaps have never done before.

- Write those activities down and spend a moment sharing and talking about them with your partner.
- Choose one or more activities that you will each do away from each other, in the spirit of celebrating yourself
- Now pull out your calendar and plot your respective activities.
- Finally, when the day(s) arrives, take a moment to remind your partner of it and show your support by saying something like... "Hey, today is your big day – I'm glad you are taking the time to be nice to yourself today – you absolutely deserve it."

Activity Ideas:
- Take a long, slow drive to somewhere you have never been. Don't plan in advance what you will do when you get there. Just take it as it comes for a whole day.
- Go shopping, do your nails, your hair, get a facial or spend a day at a spa.
- Dress up, go to a nice restaurant and order yourself a first class meal. Eat it slowly and enjoy your solitary time of self-celebration. Then treat yourself to a movie.
- Spend a day fishing or camping by yourself
- Have a whole day to yourself at your own house or apartment, Do whatever you want (no chores or work allowed) without anyone else around.
- Bake yourself a cake, decorate it with a celebratory slogan like "Happy Me Day", blow out your own candles, and eat it.
- Write a love letter to yourself about what you like and value about yourself.

- Declare a guilt-free day and eat all the stuff that you crave, watch bad TV, and pamper yourself to death.
- Go to www.beabetterpartner.com for more ideas or to share your own.

From the Real Life Archives:

Today is Your Day !!!
You have the options of :
— spending some time by yourself
✓ relaxiing in the Hot tub
— Going to the park
— Going to the Amusement Park
— Going out to dinner
— going to the movies
— Going to the Book store

Chapter 4

Swap Chores Month

We hope you are feeling nice and relaxed after "Be Good to Yourself" month, because now it's time to get down and dirty with some serious work. Well, not too serious, but yes this month involves a bit more work on your part.

More importantly, this month involves changing the way you do things. Specifically which chores you handle! It's time to abandon your definitions of "mine" and "yours" and to try some new ones on for size. That means both taking on some different responsibilities for home-related chores *and* doing the work itself differently.

Why bother? Because even though this sounds somewhat dull and unimportant, it is actually one of those things that is a real stickler in many relationships. Each partner usually takes on some very specific tasks around the apartment or house and those responsibilities rarely, if ever, change.

Debbie & Paul's Chore Swapping Anecdotes

Debbie: "When we first started working on Be A Better Partner™ I found myself looking forward to this month the most. I think I had been secretly resenting Paul's share of the chores all these years. So when we gave this month a trial run, I was amazed at how my new chore as Master Tidy-Upper took much more time than I imagined. I had been focusing on my chores in the house (you know, as the one who actually uses cleaning products) and had not given Paul much credit for all the time he spends tidying up the place on a regular basis. It wasn't easy to focus on being tidy as opposed to my version of clean, but I managed and it was certainly worth the Swap."

Paul: "When we first got married we made a pact. For the first 20 years of our marriage I would handle the bill paying and finances, and Debbie would do the cooking. For the second 20 years we have agreed to switch these roles so that Debbie will then handle the finances and I will do the cooking. The running joke around our house is that for the first 20 years we will be financially sound and eat like kings. For the second 20 years we expect to be poor and eat like crap☺."

Rather than sticking to the same routine, why not try to mix things up a bit, and wear your partner's shoes for a change? Ideally, by agreeing to shift chores you also get to shift your partnership paradigm. You get to experience what it's like doing your partner's work and have them experience what it's like doing yours. So, this month is not really about doing chores at all. It's about simple steps to assist you to better empathize with your partner and to be more appreciative of the little things they do.

Back to down and dirty, chores that is.

Steps:

1. Write down your respective household chores in two separate columns on a piece of paper.
2. Then do a little bartering and decide which of those standard chores you can swap this month. Remember to not just exchange your hard chores with your partner's easy ones. Be generous and maybe even offer to do more than an even swap.
3. Agree on which days during the month those respective swapped chores will be done.
4. Write in your chore dates on the calendar and get to work!

Activity Ideas...

- Take your partner through your chore rituals and explain what things are most important to you and why you do it the way you do. Teach them to do it your way as you go.
- Have an "anti-chore" day where you agree to just let everything go for a day and savor not having to any chores at all.
- Put a collection of your favorite songs on while you are chore swapping, and don't be afraid to dance while you work – if the spirit moves you!
- Go backwards. Start with the chores you and your partner usually do last and reverse your work order.

- Find out what chore your partner dislikes the most and volunteer to take that thing on yourself.
- Surprise your partner by doing ALL of the chores while they are away.
- Hire a cleaning service for a day as a special gift to your partner.
- Try doing your inside chores naked (with the shades drawn of course)!
- Give each other a prize, like a piece of candy or big wet one, for a chore done well or with unusual enthusiasm.
- Go to www.beabetterpartner.com for more ideas or to share your own.

From the Semi-Real Life Archives:

Chapter 5

Get in Touch with Your Feminine Side Month

Now that you have some experience trading perspectives, it's time to go all the way. During Get in Touch with Your Feminine Side Month, whoever is more masculine in the partnership will make an effort to become a little less so by trying on some more feminine habits for size. (Don't worry, your more feminine partner won't be getting off easy; they will be taking a similar challenge next month).

Just to be clear, this month's theme is not about abandoning any and all of your "manly" habits and activities. It's just about trying some new softer habits to help you get in better touch with where your partner is coming from.

What's the point in doing that? Well, we have found that in our partnership we have a tendency to adopt traditional gender roles without thinking. Sometimes those roles keep us from being open to change. Not being open to change, and not looking for opportunities to change for the better, can lead to a stagnating relationship. More importantly, by not switching things up on occasion, we can lose appreciation for all that our partner does and is on our behalf. For example, we often take it for granted that it is the other person's "job" to provide emotional support or to be the consensus builder in our relationship. By expecting our partner to take on those same roles, day in and day out, we can lose a sense of gratitude for what our partner brings to the relationship. We also abandon our individual responsibility of nurturing those positive characteristics and skills in ourselves.

This exercise will help you take a break from your self-designated roles and gain some fresh perspective and respect for your partner. It's also an opportunity to be softer on yourself in ways that you might not normally consider. So this month, let go and try getting in touch with your feminine side.

How Paul gets in Touch with his Feminine Side:

1) "I give myself permission to do something nice for myself, like taking a bath, treating myself to lunch, or getting a massage."

2) "Debbie does most of the cleaning around the house, and I tend to take care of the yard and outside work. I like to surprise her sometimes by cleaning up the house when she is away, so that she unexpectedly arrives home and it appears that the "maid" has been here. It's my small way of saying 'I appreciate what you do around here', and 'just because I am a man doesn't mean I can't do house cleaning!'"

Steps:

1. Sit with your partner and together write down - in two separate columns - the chores responsibilities and leisure activities that each of you claims on a regular basis.
2. Go through the list in each of your columns and label each of those things as "M" for masculine and "F" for feminine. Be sure to keep this list as you will be using it next month too!
3. Identify some of the key "F" responsibilities or activities and agree that this month you will switch those responsibilities to the partner who rarely if ever does them.
4. Take out your calendar and plot the specific activities on the days when one of you will get in touch with your inner feminine side.

Activity ideas:

- Take a bubble bath.
- Get a mani-pedi-facial (for you ultra masculine-types: this means a professional clean up of your finger nails, toe nails and face).
- Go to see a "Chick Flick" (bonus points if you're not afraid to cry!).
- Get a massage.
- Clean the house while your partner is away.
- Decorate your house/apartment with flowers.
- Write a love poem to your partner.
- Organize a picnic.
- Have a Girl's-Night-Out where you spend most of your time just talking to your other, more masculine friends.*

- ⓥ Commit to an "I will express my feelings" Day.
- ⓥ Give up the remote control for a week and let someone else change the channels!
- ⓥ Go to www.beabetterpartner.com for additional ideas and to share your own.

*This doesn't mean you have to force your friends to do something they don't want to do (after all we don't want you to lose all of your friends), but it wouldn't kill you to try talking about stuff that is important for a change would it?

From the Real Life Archives:

A LOVE NOTE TO DEBBIE

Coffee is nice
But YOU are nicer

Breakfast is tasty
But YOU are tastier

Sunshine is warm
But YOU are warmer

Birds chirping offer melody
But YOU are song and verse

Roses are beautiful
But YOU are the most beautiful

I LOVE YOU!!!

Chapter 6

Get in Touch with Your

Masculine Side Month

OK, time to flip the script. This month it's time to trade in some estrogen for a teaspoon or two of testosterone. During Get in Touch with Your Masculine Side month, whoever is more feminine in the partnership will experiment with becoming a bit more masculine.

Just like last month, this month's theme is not about abandoning any and all of your feminine habits and activities. It's just about trying some new, "manly" habits to help you get in better touch with where your partner is coming from.

A reminder as to why this is important...we have found that in a partnership we have a tendency to adopt certain roles without thinking. Sometimes those roles keep us from being open to change. Not being open to change, and not looking for opportunities to change for the better, can lead to a stagnating relationship. More importantly, by not switching things up on occasion, we can lose appreciation for all that our partner does and is on our behalf. For example, we often take it for granted that it is the other person's "job" to make the important decisions or to fix things around the house, etc. By expecting our partner to take on those same roles, day in and day out, we can lose a sense of gratitude for what our partner brings to the relationship. We also abandon our individual responsibility for nurturing those positive characteristics and skills in ourselves.

If you don't often take a break and switch your self-designated roles, here is your opportunity to do so while gaining fresh perspective and heightened appreciation of your partner. It's also an opportunity to be nice to yourself in ways that you don't normally do. So this month let loose and try beating your chest a little and have fun getting in touch with your masculine side.

How Debbie gets in Touch with her Masculine Side:

1) "Paul puts a lot of work into our yard, so once in a while when he's not around, I try to surprise him by doing some of the grunt work, like mowing the grass or trimming the hedges."

2) "Once in a while, I try to take on a fix-it project of my own. I can't say I am always able to complete it by myself (like the time I decided to put in a new bathroom sink!), but I do my homework, ask questions at the home improvement store, and dedicate myself to learning something new. And regardless of how well I do, inevitably, I've managed to boost my self-esteem a bit."

Steps:

   1. Sit down with your partner and take a minute to talk about what you learned last month, when one of you attempted to get in better touch with your feminine side.

2. Pull out the list you made last month in which you identified chores, responsibilities and leisure activities as "M" for masculine and "F" for feminine. If you haven't yet made an "M" list, do it now.
3. Identify some of the key "M" responsibilities or activities and agree that this month you will switch those responsibilities to the partner who rarely if ever does them.
4. Take out your calendar and plot the specific activities on the days when one of you will get in touch with your inner masculine side.
5. Let the chest beating begin!

Activity ideas:
- Go to an auto race or monster truck show.
- Hang out at a biker bar.
- Spend some time working on your car.
- Forego talking about your feelings for a day – or focus on talking less for one whole day.
- Watch a sports game – either on TV or live.
- Have a "fix it" day working around your home.
- Cook a meal on a BBQ grill.
- Go fishing.
- Learn how to use power tools.
- Wear boxers.
- Go to www.beabetterpartner.com for additional ideas or to share your own.

From the Real Life Archives:

Chapter 6½

Take a Moment to Reflect

and Celebrate

Before you move on to Month 7, you should congratulate yourself and your partner for half a year of hard work. You have come a long way in just 6 months, and hopefully had a good time doing it?

Before you move on to the next half of the year and the rest of your life together, we encourage you to take a moment to reflect on how things have gone so far. Anything different in your relationship as a result of your efforts to be a better partner one month at a time? Talk about it, share what you have learned, and get ready for more challenges and fun ahead.

More importantly, before you turn the page and move into month seven, do something to celebrate your successes thus far. (Note: for this one you don't need to pull out your calendar...just do it!)

Celebration Ideas:

- ⦿ Give each other a long, sexy kiss, and...well you know the rest.
- ⦿ Pat each other on the back, literally, by exchanging massages.
- ⦿ Get dressed up and go out for a nice dinner.
- ⦿ Take a drive together and just enjoy some quality time together.
- ⦿ Put on "your song" and dance, dance, dance.
- ⦿ Bake a We-are-Better-Partners cake.
- ⦿ Put a secret note under your partner's pillow or somewhere for them to find, that describes how much they mean to you.
- ⦿ Pull out a bottle of bubbly and toast each other.
- ⦿ Go to www.beabetterpartner.com and share your "dos" and "don'ts" with other couples.

Chapter 7

Work Less Month

All the role swapping can really wear a partner out. So it's time to take a break. Literally, this month is about working less and relaxing more. The point of Work Less Month is not just about taking time to enjoy yourself more, which is a good thing in and of itself. More importantly it's about using that extra time to be with and value your partner.

The more time you make available for each other, the more you put your relationship front and center. It's also an important reminder of who you are really working for, that is, each other and your family.

Of course, by working less we don't mean to suggest that you shouldn't work at all (or get fired in the process of working less), but that you make a special effort beyond your usual vacation time to carve out some space for each other. It's all about working less to enjoy each other and what you have together even more. Take some time out and put some time in...to your partnership.

Debbie and Paul's Work Less Experiences:

Debbie: "For a long time, I was so proud of myself for choosing a partner who didn't have an addictive personality (an area of concern for me). But then I realized, he does have an addiction – work! I rushed out and bought a book on the subject right away. After reading it, I encouraged Paul to read it too. I thought that if he could realize that he had a problem, we could work it out. But, I knew all I could do was work on my own issues surrounding my new reality. So I stopped bugging him about coming home late from work, and I found some hobbies of my own (not work!) and...voila....every year it gets much easier."

Paul: "After Debbie and I had first moved in together, we hit a major speed bump in our relationship. Driving to work one morning we got into a major argument and a little voice inside me said 'you either have to deal with this now or the gig is up'. Even though I had a really busy day at work that day, and I am a workaholic by nature, I pulled off the road and into a park so that we could sit down and talk. I called in sick to work and we spent a good couple of hours talking and working things out. I think that one, simple action may have saved our relationship."

Steps:

1. Sit down and take a minute to talk about your current work schedules and how much time you devote to each other on a weekly or monthly basis.
2. Then think about how you might free up some time this month for each other.
3. Pull out your wall calendar or access your electronic calendar and plot some specific days/times when you will scale back your work (both professional and household work) and devote that time to joint activities.
4. Keep reminding each other this month that you don't live to work: You work to live!

Activity Ideas:

- Call in sick one day and have a date day with your partner.
- Come home early from work one day and surprise your partner with a gift, dinner, or a backrub.
- Have a "chore less" weekend when you don't worry about all the little stuff and instead plan fun activities together at home.
- When you are at work take 5 minutes to close your door, close your eyes, take deep breaths, and think about your partner and something nice you might do for them.
- Take an additional day off over a long weekend and plan a partner's day.
- Trade the time you usually devote to a non-essential chore (like vacuuming or washing the car) for some partner quality time.
- Try doing your chores together instead of separately.

- Take a long lunch during one work day, and enjoy it with your partner.
- Agree to keep the computer off one night a week or one day every weekend.
- Grab a piece of paper and write down how great you feel after you've spent time on doing something other than chores or work.
- Go to www.beabetterpartner.com for additional ideas or to share your own.

From the Real Life Archives:

Deb:

Sorry for abandoning you last night.

Tonight I am here!

Would you like to:

(A) TALK ?

(B) Vent ?

(C) Read ?

(D) play GAMES ?

(E) fool around ?

(F) Party like it's 1999

Chapter 8

Stop Driving Me Crazy Month

Hopefully you are now better rested from working less, because this month is going to involve some additional energy. It's time to pay full attention to, and to do something about, what gets under your partner's skin.

No matter how good our relationship with our partner is, there are always things that bug us about each other. This is perfectly normal and to be expected - unless, of course, you are clones of each other. Even if you are good about telling each other what bugs you, and even if you are good at responding to it, there is always room for improvement. So let's take a little time this month to see if we can address each others pet peeves in a way that in and of itself won't drive you crazy. Let's be honest with each other, get a few things off of our chests, and set the tone for more easily clearing out future "you-drive-me-crazy" landmines in the relationship.

Rather than just dumping all of your dislikes out on the table all at once, instead we urge you to take one pet peeve at a time. This way it doesn't seem like you have just been waiting in the wings for an opportunity to jump all over your partner for their past transgressions against your person. We also suggest you *don't* start your conversations with "you drive me crazy when you...". Instead of offering a proverbial punch to the gut, you might want to try a lighter touch. For example, try starting with the statement, "You know, I would really love it if you didn't do...anymore". In our experience, this approach seems to get much better results.

Finally, it may also be helpful to remember that your partner may not have known how much certain things bugged you if you didn't tell them...or if you told them in a way that ended up driving them crazy.

So take a couple of deep breaths, look your partner right in the eye, and tell them how to drive you...sane!

Steps:

1. Sit down and take some time to have an honest conversation, giving equal time to each other, about things that your partner does which bug you.
2. Select the things that are most important to each of you and make a pledge that you will work hard to change those things this month.
3. Pull out your wall calendar or access your electronic calendar and write down a series of reminders and/or activities to help keep you on track.
4. When you come across a reminder during the month, be sure to ask your partner if they still feel bugged. If the honest answer is yes, then ask "What could I be doing differently or better?" Then do it!

Debbie and Paul's Stop Driving Me Crazy Examples:

Debbie: "I'll never forget one of our first fights, while driving on vacation. As the Navigator, I was in charge of interpreting our maps and I remember Paul asking me how long it would take us to drive from Atlanta to Savannah and I said 'it looks like about 2-3 hours'. Since this was before the invention of maps online, I really had no idea. So I was amazed when he actually got angry with me after three hours in the car, that we weren't even close to arriving. It was then that I realized how goal-oriented and focused Paul could be – and that it would really help him if I could be more specific and take more ownership of my job as Navigator when we are traveling."

Paul: "Debbie had this habit of taking leftovers that are no longer good out of the refrigerator and putting them into the sink. Instead of emptying the food out of their containers and washing them she often left it there for someone else (me) to deal with. After years of driving me nuts with this habit, we finally addressed it and I learned that she was really trying to let me know that she wanted me to pitch in and take responsibility for cleaning out the refrigerator too. So now I make a point of pitching in and she no longer leaves leftovers in the sink for me to take care of."

Activity Ideas:
- Trade chores and responsibilities that you most dislike (and perhaps are feeling resentful about) with your partner.
- When your partner makes us a conscious effort to change something that bugs you, follow it with a hug and a kiss (or something more passionate☺).

- Make Crazy lists & post them for each other. Leave room for writing the date and a thank-you note when your partner makes an effort NOT to bug you.
- Give your partner a dollar every time they change a habit that irritates you.
- Treat yourself to a reward after you make the effort to change an irritating habit.
- Plan an "I Will Drive You Sane Day" with your partner, where you both make a huge effort to do "bug free things" that make for household happiness.
- Talk to your partner as soon as you see them doing something that bugs you. Don't wait and let it simmer. Start the conversation with something like, "Hey, I would really appreciate it if you..." or "I know you don't mean to bug me, but when you do _____ it drives me nuts."
- Go to www.beabetterpartner.com for additional ideas or to share your own.

From the Real Life Archives:

How I can
Stop making
Paul nuts!

1. Be more _tidy!_
2. Don't impose on his quiet time
3. Stick to our agreements (like budgets #)
4. Buy more licorice
5. Read & write more.
6. Stop interrupting

How to stop driving
Debbie Crazy

① Be more present
② clean off the kitch sink
③ Be an equal partner in child care responsibilities
④ Empty out the fridge
⑤ Talk as much as you listen
⑥ Don't use metal on pans

Chapter 9

Listen or Be Heard Month

Now that things are a bit less crazy, we think you are ready for something challenging. During Listen or Be Heard Month you will be having some fun working on your communication skills.

In most couples' relationships there tends to be one person that does less talking and one person that does more. So, this month our goal is to give a little more voice and expression to the quiet partner and a little more of a listening ear to the partner who does most of the talking. For example, instead of the "talker" expecting the "listener" to hear all about their day after coming home from work, the Talker should first ask a question like "Tell me how YOU are doing?"

Conversely, the "listener" should try to spend more time this month talking about things that are important to them or expressing their feelings about something they care about but don't often bring up. Of course, when your "silent" partner is talking you need to encourage them by shutting up. And, for you serial listeners, remember that people will only listen if you work hard at having something to say.

If you both are talkers or both are listeners, then your goal this month is to try and do the opposite of what you normally do.

Why bother taking the time to better listen or be heard? Because in our experience, a fun and thriving relationship is all about communicating better and often, and even small changes in our usual habits can make big changes in the relationship.

This month is **NOT** about trying to change your respective personalities, but about challenging yourselves to try to be better listeners and talkers. So open your ears and mouths, and see if you don't open your minds and hearts more in the process.

Steps:

1. Sit down and talk about who tends to do most of the talking and who does the listening in the partnership. (Hint: It might be a good idea for the more reserved partner to start the conversation☺)
2. Then discuss how you might change things up a bit this month and reverse talker/listener roles in a way that can enhance your communication.
3. Dust off your wall calendar or whip out your electronic calendar and plot some specific activities for Listen or Be Heard month.
4. Be sure to have the more passive partner get in the last word in this conversation.

Debbie and Paul's Favorite Listen or Be Heard Examples:

Debbie: "It always amazes me, when I ask Paul to tell me about his day. For years, he would simply say "fine." Finally, one day I asked him if he could use more words to describe his day. It took a while, but eventually he seemed to understand what I meant. So, now, when he gets all quiet on me - all I have to do is say 'more words please' and we both laugh and he starts REALLY talking. We also had a great discussion about how he didn't think I'd be interested in the minutiae of his day, whereas I was really feeling abandoned rather than bogged down."

Paul: "Debbie comes from a loud family and I come from a quieter branch of the species. Needless to say she does a lot more talking and I tend to be quieter...especially when I am pissed off about something. So over the years I have learned to speak up and not let things simmer to the boiling point. One other habit that helps both of us is prefacing comments with 'I feel like...'. This tends to get Debbie's attention and let's her know that I have something important to say. And it doesn't put her on the defensive if I am unhappy about something she did."

Activity Ideas:

- ◉ Take 5 minutes during dinner or in the evening to report with equal time on how each other's day went.
- ◉ Have a "Feelings" day each week where you challenge each other to express how you are feeling emotionally (NOT physically). Start and end these days with the phrase "right now I feel...".

- Have a no talk morning or afternoon, where you both practice the lost art of shutting up and being OK with a little silence.
- Turn off the TV one night a week and talk about your family, your personal hopes, dreams, and challenges.
- On your next date night don't go to the movies or a play. Instead take a walk or go have coffee and just talk.
- Try turning your radio off and putting your MP3 player away for a day and just listen to the sounds all around you.
- Have an "I am completely present for you Day". No reading, no radio/TV or computers. Just people to people interactions.
- Have a party at your house and let your quieter half do the hosting for a change.
- Sit in the movie theater or in your car after the movie and talk about what you liked or didn't like and how the movie made you feel.
- Come up with a hand signal that let's your partner know when you need to have some quiet time. Conversely, come up with a hand signal that let's your partner know when you really need to talk and be heard.
- If you are uncomfortable talking about your feelings at first, start by writing it in a letter or email to your partner.
- Go to www.beabetterpartner.com for additional ideas or to share your own.

From the Real Life Archives:

Dear Paul—
I don't know how to tell you everything I am feeling but I don't want to take it for granted that you know. So here goes....

Chapter 10

Parent Role Reversal Month

Are you ready for another switcheroo? This month the focus will be on trying to better understand and appreciate the role of your partner as a parent. In order to do that you are encouraged to switch some of the roles and responsibilities that you and your partner typically undertake or have traditionally assigned to each other. If you don't have kids (or a pet) then use this month to try switching general roles and responsibilities in the world that you and your partner share.

The reason to attempt yet another walking-a-mile-in-your-Partner's-shoes is, as you experienced in Chapters 4,5, and 6, to gain some better perspective and insight into what they experience on a day to day basis. As a result you may see parenting in a different and more complete light – in a way that pays tribute to the amazing partnership required for parenting. Second, a reminder that it never hurts to switch up your daily routine, so as to keep things fresh in your relationship and avoid the drudgery of "unchange".

When swapping some of your roles and responsibilities as parents (or partners), be sure to start small and work your way up. For example, don't immediately hand over all "Mommy" duties over to "Daddy" and vice versa in one fell swoop. The goal of this month is not to change you into what you are not - or have not chosen to be – but instead to get a taste of what your partner does and thereby honor it and them. Have fun with your exchange and even try out some new ways of parenting that you can role model for your partner. Who knows, you might even become better parents as a result?

Steps:

1. Sit down and explore how you view your respective roles and responsibilities as parents (or partners in general).
2. Make a quick list of your respective parenting (or partner) duties.
3. Pull out your wall calendar or access your electronic calendar and select a series of days where you will switch some of those duties. Write down the specific days and specific responsibilities that you will switch.
4. Tell each other that you know it won't be easy to get out of your current parenting (or partnering) comfort zone, but that you will do your best out of respect for each other.
5. Jump in and enjoy the chance to try out some new parenting roles and ideas.

Debbie and Paul's Parent Role Reversal Examples:

Debbie: "It's important to me that I try to be a 'Fun Mommy' like my own mother was for me. Yet it always seemed to me that Paul was the one who was out at the park or the pool every weekend playing with the girls while I ran errands. So, one Saturday, I decided it was time for me to switch roles and to be the parent I really wanted to be – the fun one as I saw in Paul - and surprise everyone by joining them at the neighborhood pool. I was surprised at what a difference it made in everyone, that I dropped my Saturday chores to have FUN, just like Daddy does."

Paul: "When I began working part-time a couple of years ago so that I could spend part of the day with our kids, I also took on a new responsibility of dressing and doing the hair for our two little girls. Normally I have enough of a challenge just dressing myself, so trying to figure out how to match (or determine front and back) for those little girly outfits pushed me to the limit. If that wasn't enough, I had to figure out how to do pony tails and braids and all of those other crazy hair things that are listed in some secret Mommy handbook. Well, my kids still don't look very good when I dress them (you can tell instantly which one of us dressed and groomed them), but I have gotten better at it. More importantly, I really do appreciate all of the TLC that Debbie puts into making our girls look great."

Activity Ideas:

- Pick one day out of the week as parent role reversal day and switch major parenting responsibilities. If one parent is doing it all, then that parent can either take the day off or assist the other in getting up to speed on responsibilities that they need help with.
- Ask your kids (or your talking pets) what they like about how each of you do certain things and then tell them that you need their help with a game where you will be changing responsibilities. The winner will be the parent who is most creative and has the most fun with various parenting responsibilities that are swapped. Let your kids choose the winner.
- Take a day off from work and spend it with your kids doing a series of new things. This is a good way to get them primed for you taking on different parenting responsibilities and a good thing in itself!
- Shadow your partner during a particular day and learn how he or she handles various parenting responsibilities. Give (and take) suggestions as you go.
- Take turns being in charge at the dinner table. The parent not in charge that night gets to relax and observe.
- Ask your kids what they like about the opposite parent. Try to integrate those same characteristics into your own parenting.
- Tell your partner what you most like about their parenting.

- Share with each other the most important things you learned from your own parents about parenting.
- Reward each other for taking the time to try on a new parenting hat.
- Go to www.beabetterpartner.com for additional ideas or to share your own.

From the Real Life Archives:

Debbie:

I am taking the girls to get their hair cut — and I may even get one myself!

But I won't be getting their nails done (or mine). A guy's gotta have a little self respect :)

Love, — Rob

Chapter 11

Togetherness Month

This month is all about putting aside some quality time to be together. You may be thinking you can skip this month because you two are already together all the time. That may be the case, but how much of that time together do you spend really enjoying and appreciating one another? The correct answer is "it's never enough". The person that you have chosen as your partner deserves every bit of your attention, and here's an opportunity to show it.

During Togetherness Month we encourage you both to take additional time to be together physically and emotionally (and spiritually if you are so inclined). It doesn't require that you take a big vacation to the Bahamas or to send the kids off to boarding school. It simply requires you to carve out some extra time at home or elsewhere and to commit that time to being with each other.

Ideally you will use this extra time to do fun, romantic, couples stuff. But you could just as easily spend the time hanging out watching a movie or playing golf. The important thing is that you do it together and commit to being fully present for your partner at that time. Laugh together, be serious together, dance together, or sit on your front porch together. It doesn't matter what you do...as long as you do it together with a capital "T".

Debbie and Paul's Favorite Togetherness Activities:

Debbie: "In order to save money recently, we decided to cancel our subscription to the newspaper. When that happened, Paul started sitting at the computer every morning reading the newspaper and I really missed our time together. After some discussion, it was an easy adjustment to have Paul bring his laptop into the living room with me and read his news there, instead of alone in the office – and I didn't feel abandoned on Sunday mornings anymore!"

Paul: "One of my favorite things to do is to "camp out" right in our own house. In other words we take our sleeping bags into the living room or sleep somewhere else in the house other than in our own bed. It's a kind of mini adventure that gets us out of our comfort zone and allows us to be more creative and playful with each other." (Note: this activity is not recommended if you have a bad back!)

Steps:

1. Take a minute to talk about your favorite things to do together. Talk about what you each most enjoy and why. Also brainstorm about some fun things to do together that you haven't yet tried
2. Pull out your wall calendar or access your electronic calendar and write in some together activities that you can commit to this month.

3. Every morning this month when you rise think about how you can spend just a little extra time together that day.
4. All together now...have fun and enjoy hanging out with the person you are closest to in the world.

Activity Ideas:

- If you sleep in the same bed, snuggle up close to each other and try watching TV or reading this way.
- Accompany your partner to do something that they normally do alone or with others.
- Try a new couple's hobby like dancing, roller skating, or crafts.
- Take a bath or shower together.
- Rent a movie that shows couples having fun together.
- Rent a bicycle built for two and go on a picnic.
- Drive or commute to work together.
- Instead of watching TV in bed at night, play a board game together.
- Read to each other in bed.
- Make a point of holding hands when you are out and about.
- Take an in-town vacation and get a room at a nearby hotel/motel.
- Go to www.beabetterpartner.com for additional ideas or to share your own.

From the Real Life Archives:

Chapter 12

Lighten Up Month

You've come a long way, baby! You have both done a great job so far and now you are finally on the home stretch. But rather than dig in for the last lap, we suggest that you slow down and take it easy. In fact, you both need to just LIGHTEN UP!

Rather than adding to your already busy load we want you to leave this final month feeling good (if not great) about your relationship with your significant other. That doesn't mean you have the month off. On the contrary, you have the month ON when it comes to your partnership, but in a way that is meant to keep a smile on your faces.

In our experience the only thing worse than not trying at all is trying too hard to make a relationship work. As a result you can end up missing the forest through the trees. The fact that you have gone through the whole year attempting to Be a Better Partner™ means that you are indeed committed. So take this time to celebrate your successes. Instead of celebrating with a specific reward, celebrate with a simple laugh, a squeeze of the hand, or an unexpected tickling. The best reward you could possibly have is a happier, more spontaneous relationship, where your togetherness comes naturally.

So, your mission this month is not to take yourselves or your relationship too seriously. By that we mean use your together time for fun, silly, and unconventional activities. Don't worry about whether they are the right thing to do, just go with it and see what happens. Lighten up with each other, and see if your life doesn't do the same.

Debbie and Paul's Lighten Uppers

Debbie: *"I used to joke with my friend, Keith, that when things got hectic, I would mentally remind myself that I could choose to WATCH the 'Crazy Parade' rather than be a participant in the parade of craziness that we sometimes call Life. Then, one day I woke up and suddenly realized that I could actually reduce my own stress level in really simple ways. For example, when having friends over for dinner - I could actually finish cleaning the house 30 minutes BEFORE everyone arrived, and sit down and relax until the party started. Wow, what a difference that simple commitment made in my life - as it rolled over into other areas, like work, the holiday season, etc. I may still be a bit Type A" but I'm much closer to a B+ these days."*

Paul: *"Sometimes when I am really stressed out, I worsen my condition by trying to do more work and make myself feel more productive. Debbie is really good at reminding me not to take myself so seriously. Thanks to her suggestion, I now take the night off when I get crazy stressed. I usually sit in bed and watch bad TV and eat bad food. Nine times out of ten I feel much better the next morning - minus the stomach ache☺."*

Steps:

1. Take a couple of deep breaths, and put all of the busyness out of your minds.
2. Talk about how and when you both need to lighten up. What things, both this month and in general, stress you out and how can you make some slight changes to avoid those stresses?
3. Get specific and come up with some activities this month that will help you both to lighten up. (Note: try planning lighten up activities just before or after the stressful things happening this month)
4. Take another deep breath, say to yourselves: "We NEED to lighten up and we WILL lighten up". Then see if you can levitate off the ground☺

Activity Ideas:

- Plan less holiday activities this year, and use the extra time to do fun, together stuff.
- Do your holiday planning together, spreading out the responsibilities more equally.
- Plan a Lighten Up Day where you goof off, watch funny movies, and do lots and lots of tickling and practical jokes.
- Buy one less present this year, and give the money instead to a charity or a needy neighborhood family in the name of your loved one. This will lighten your load and lighten someone else's as well!
- Look at yourselves in the mirror every morning or evening and try to make each other laugh with funny faces or a joke.

- Count to 10 before you are about to fly off the handle and start screaming at your significant other. Think "I am light as a feather" or "I am a cool breeze".
- Give each other a big hug before bed at night and say: "Everything is going to be just fine".
- Learn a few new jokes and try them out on each other.
- Get rid of some of the clutter in your house or apartment so as to feel "lighter".
- Section off one part of your weekends or weeknights – and commit to refusing to schedule anything within that block of time. Then do it again the next weekend!
- Go to www.beabetterpartner.com for additional ideas or to share your own.

From the Real Life Archives:

It's Not your responsibility!
You're wonderful!
It is what it is!
It's going to be ok!
You can do it!
Don't Give Up! Hang in there!

Chapter 13

An After-Word

CONGRATULATIONS on a whole year of being a better partner! How did it go? Do you feel any differently about each other? What did you learn? Do you feel any closer than you were before the year began? Most importantly: DID YOU HAVE FUN?

We are very curious to learn about your experiences, so that we can make improvements and share your ideas with other couples. Please take a minute and go to www.beabetterpartner.com to the online community page and tell us your story, share your ideas, and recommend activities and services for other couples. It's all about sharing the love!

We hope that the Be A Better Partner™ program has offered you a useful tool in improving your relationship. We also hope that you have been able to put some more fun into your relationship. Finally, we hope that you are feeling renewed and excited about the years ahead together.

Some parting advice, if we can be so bold:

- Focus on what you have together, NOT what you don't own, or think you are lacking as persons.
- Play silly and often.
- Be creative in your relationship.
- Don't be afraid to ask for help if you need it. Be OK with the possibility that you need more help than this or any other book or program can provide. Seriously consider a professional therapist or psychologist for the big stuff.
- Take time for each other. You and your relationship are worth it!
- Keep working at your relationship. But remember that work can be fun.

Blessings & Happiness!

Paul & Debbie Lamb
- Lambs On Love

Your Activity Ideas

Your Activity Ideas

Your Activity Ideas

Your Activity Ideas

2292171

Made in the USA